I SURVIVED MY NARC

THE GREAT ESCAPE

FELICIA CARR

This book is dedicated to my Mother Rosa Lee Wysinger who transitioned before this book was published. Unbeknownst to her she gave me every tool that I ever needed in life to get through this ordeal and make it out with a sane mind and whole body, if it were not for her, I would not have been able to make it out and be the women I am today. I pray to have made her proud with every decision that I made and every step that I took to be a better me. I will always be grateful for the strong women that she was and for everything that she did for me to ensure that I had a successful future. If it were not for her, I do not know where I would have been in life she showed me to never depend on anyone and to go get it. You do not know what you do not know, until you know!

Finally, my daughter, my Studmuffin, My Rider, my everything the one person who has loved me through every stage of this journey with no judgment and no questions. You were there when no one else was there, you were there to listen to all those plans with no judgement. You gave me something to push for, you gave me reason to push through even on days that I did not feel like it. I pray that I am everything that you have envisioned a mother to be because you are 1000% everything that I imagined a daughter to be and more. I love you to the moon and back and I am so proud of you.

Table of Contents

How to Safely Escape and Abusive Relationship

Chapter 1
The Great Escape
Felicia Carr

Born and raised in the city of Oakland, California, 1976 was the year, May 19th to be exact. I was the youngest of four and the only girl so I had no clue what the years ahead of me would look like.

Growing up, Oakland was the city of the pimps, players, hustlers and everything in between. Luckily, I never fell victim to any of the things that were happening around me. My mother kept a tight hold on me and I will forever be grateful for everything that she kept me away from. Not only was I the youngest of four and the only girl, I came along 10 years after my last sibling. My late addition proved to mold me into the woman who stands before you today.

Growing up under 3 brothers, I had a firsthand experience of who and what I did not want in a spouse and there were certain things that I knew I would not settle for. I never saw a healthy relationship between a man and a woman. I just knew what I did not want. I was raised around a lot of settling; the women settled for what the men gave, and they were content. I knew that was not the dynamic I wanted for my life. I grew up strong willed and did not take any shit from anybody so I thought I had it all figured out until I met the love of my life in 2015, or so I thought……

January 17, 2015, was a day that unbeknownst to me would change my life forever. It was a Saturday night and I had decided to go to Geoffrey's Inner Circle, a spot in Oakland with food, drinks and live music. As soon as I walked in, I saw a tall, dark handsome man standing to the side as I passed by. He smiled, I smiled back and I kept walking. I had no idea what was about to unfold. A few days prior to that, his cousin put up a Facebook post with a picture of him and I commented on it, not knowing that I would run into this person a few days later. I didn't recognize him at the club but someone who saw the post told me who he was and went up to him to tell him who I was, but he already knew me, we went to high school together and he remembered me so that's where the story takes off.

 Two days later, he found me on Facebook, inboxed me, and the rest is history. A week in and we were texting and talking nonstop. He came to stay the night at my place and a few days later, I went to stay the night with him and never went back home. It was a match made in Heaven, so I thought. The chemistry was crazy from the very beginning, and I thought I had found my person. I stayed with him for nine months and then we finally decided to get a place together. We both packed up our places and became one. At the time, his oldest son was living with him and shortly after he got his youngest son too. Overall, things were good, a few hiccups here and there but nothing major; we were adjusting to our blended family.

Things were great, but I was not prepared for what was ahead......

Now, let's fast forward to September 2017. I went on a trip to Dubai. When I came back, things changed. All of a sudden, marriage was the topic of conversation and on October 24, 2017, we said, "I do" in a small, private ceremony with 12 of our closest family members and friends. Things were good until he got a wild hair up his ass and decided he wanted to expand the family. He already had four children and I had one adult daughter. I had made it very clear that I was done having children yet, here we were, having this conversation so of course I entertained the idea. After all, he was my husband, right?

Due to my age, I could not conceive naturally. After many tests, the final result was that in order for us to have a baby together, I would have to get a donor egg and have it implanted inside of me. Technically, it wouldn't be my child, it would be his with another woman. I would only be the carrier. I really wasn't feeling that considering that I didn't want any more children anyway. At this point, we had three of his children living with us. Little did I know, all hell was about to break lose and he was trying to throw another child into the already hectic situation. It became an absolute NO for me. That's when things took a turn and he could no longer hide behind the mask; his true colors started to emerge and that would be the beginning of the end. The next two years were a living hell. Knowing what I know now, the Narcissist hates to be told NO so that is when his true self came out.

That's when I began to notice that he lacked accountability. He was always the victim in every situation. He was cocky, had no self-control and was arrogant. The worst was the controlling behavior. He tried to control what I wore, where I went, and who I went with. He was very calculated in the way that he went about it. It started with little remarks, then whenever I said I had plans, he would all of sudden have plans for us that somehow always fell through once I cancelled my original plans.

I'm very respectful in how I dress and how I carry myself so it took me by surprise when he tried to control what I wore. That's when I really began to notice the shift in his demeanor, once I no longer adhered to his rules per say. He could no longer hide who he was and his representative was long gone. The real him was in rare form. He thought he had me locked in, but little did he know. This girl from East Oakland that was raised under three brothers and a mother, who I never saw be mistreated or disrespected by a man, was going to show him what he was up against.

Fast forward to 2019, he was still badgering me about a baby. I wasn't coming off of my NO and it was killing him. At that point, I realized that he clearly wanted a baby more than he wanted a wife because I was adamant about not having a baby. At the time, his youngest was 14 and we were four years away from being empty nesters. I was done having children and was ready to live our best, peaceful life and travel, but he couldn't take no for an answer and that's when it all started to fall apart. I didn't give in to his demands and in his mind "What wife would not want to give their husband a child?" He would say it every chance he got!

Knowing what I know now, that was the beginning of the manipulation stage and it was going downhill fast. I told him every step of the way where I was within the marriage and after awhile, I started to check out mentally. I started falling out of love with him. I was no longer sexually attracted to him and I told him every step of the way how I felt. Still, he would not budge from wanting a baby. It was so bad that I told him to go have a baby with someone else since that seemed to be his only concern. In hindsight, it had nothing to do with a baby, it was all about control. If I would have given in and gave him a child, I would not have been able to leave him so easily and he knew it.

Here is where it gets tricky. It's 2020 and COVID hits. Now the world was shut down and we were all stuck in the house together 24/7, sounds fun, right? Fuck no! 2020 was horrible! Imagine being stuck in the house with someone that you are consistently battling with, it's no fun so in May 2020, I made the decision to move out. I got a place, and he felt something was happening but didn't know what. It was almost as if a light bulb popped on in his head so he brought up the idea of therapy. I had been asking him to go for a year and he would always say, "No, I'm not the one with the problem, you are, so I don't need to go." Something in him changed when he found out I was moving; he found a Black Male Therapist and we started counseling.

The therapist started with him solo and then met with me solo. We had the third session together and that is when it happened, I finally had someone agreeing with me and I was not crazy! Our therapist told him "You are going to lose your wife!" And he was right, but he did not want to take any advice from him so needless to say, that was our last therapy session with him. Then he decided he wanted me to pick the therapist so I picked a white woman. I wanted the total opposite of what we had previously. 20 minutes into our session, she laughed and said to him, "You have a very twisted way of thinking!" She immediately apologized and stated that her reaction was very unprofessional. However, the things that came out of his mouth would shock anybody. Needless to say, that was our last visit with her so we were back at square one.

Later, I was sitting in bed when a friend of mine opened up to me about her situation with her husband. Some of what she said reminded me of my story. She told me to get a book called "Becoming the Narcissist's Worst Nightmare," written by Shahida Arabi. I finally began to realize that I was not crazy and for years I thought I was losing my mind. In reality, the manipulation, mind games and gas lighting will have you thinking you are crazy. Trust me you are not crazy, it is them! It was not until I read the book that I started to learn about narcissism and quickly realized that I was indeed married to one and he would never change. In May of 2020, I planned a 2 week visit to Houston and he flew to be with me for the second half of the trip. We drove up to Dallas I remember being so unhappy.

I knew I had to take my life back and I decided to move to Houston, Texas. I knew I was going with or without him and I made that very clear! I was over it! I was stressed out, losing weight, and sadly, I had lost myself. I looked in the mirror one day and didn't recognize the person that was looking back at me. Enough was enough, it was time for change! I voiced my concerns to him and he promised that he would get help and do better. I trusted what he said, hell he was my husband, so I put my faith in him and on November 1, 2020, we moved to Houston. The move was complete and seven months into living what was supposed to be our best new life in Houston, this move would prove to be the biggest mistake ever! There was absolutely no change at all.

I remember the day like it was yesterday, we were standing in our room and he was arguing with me; I had no fight left in me. I used to always say "I'm done, I'm over this marriage, I want a divorce" and in the midst of his rant, I remember holding onto my Amethyst (Protection) crystal necklace that my cousin had given me right before we left. I said, 'I'm done" and his reply was ,"You keep saying that you are done and yo ass ain't left yet, you're still here." It was at that very moment that I vowed to never say it again. I vowed to just MOVE IN SILENCE and that's exactly what I did. He thought he had me but I had something up my sleeve for his ass. "Operation let me show him that fat meat is greasy" was in full swing.

It was June 2021, I knew it wouldn't be easy and I knew he wasn't going to just let me leave in peace. When you know what type of person you are dealing with then you plan accordingly. Even though he had never been physical, you never know what a person will do when they feel like their back is against a wall. I had no plan at first, I just knew I needed to leave. I knew I didn't want to go into the New Year with him and I thought about our seven-year anniversary of being together. Seven means completion and I did not want to complete that journey. I understood the assignment! I learned my lesson and it was time for me to get off of that rollercoaster ride. By this time, it was only him and I living in a 3,200 square foot house and I was absolutely miserable. Here is where it gets good, where the actual planning starts.......

October 2021

My first plan was to leave him on October 24th which was our four-year wedding anniversary. I knew that would sting every year, however, I needed more time. I picked my "Freedom Date" 12-1-21, that date reads the same frontwards and backwards. I told the few people who needed to know, and I started planning. I had all the bases covered, there was no way this plan could fail! Since it was only us, I came up with the idea of moving into a 1-bedroom apartment to save money and stack to buy a house, so I literally sold everything in the house except for our bedroom set. We had put it in storage and were just sleeping on our mattress on the floor.

We went to view apartments together with me knowing full well that we would never move into one but I had to do what I had to do to execute the plan and to make sure it went off without a hitch. It had to work, my life depended on it.

November rolled around and I was 30 days away from my big escape. I tried to ensure that the rest of my stay was as peaceful as possible. There was tons of agreeing and biting my tongue, I just wanted out. I hated everything about this man, the way he walked, talked and everything in between and I knew that I could no longer allow myself to be a vessel for his pleasure. I knew I couldn't take another day of allowing him to jump up and down on me.

The very last time I tried to engage in intercourse with him was awful! It was at that time that I was able to truly understand how sexual assault victims got through the assault; you have to mentally check out and that's where I was at. The last time we tried to be intimate my intrusive thoughts kicked in and I blurted out "Why is this taking so long?" I realized that I said it out loud and not in my mind by the look on his face. That was the last time I ever allowed him to be one with me, I was over it!

It was at that time that I came up with the brilliant idea of telling him about a "30-day sex cleanse." He took the bait and it worked. I couldn't wrap my mind around allowing him to become one with me another day. Thank God he fell for it. If my mind wasn't feeling it, then the rest of my body wouldn't either.

The following day, I made him a dentist appointment for 2:50 p.m. on 12/1/21. I knew he would be there at least 2 hours since it was his first visit. My plan was falling into place.......

I had to stick it out with him from October to December. It was hard! There were times when I would cry myself to sleep. Some nights, I would be in the bathroom crying and praying to God to give me a sign that I was in fact doing the right thing by leaving because granted, this was my husband. One night, I logged into Facebook, and I saw that I was tagged in a post titled, "Signs of Emotional Abuse." There was a list of 15 signs and he checked 14 of the 15 listed. I had never talked to the person that tagged me but, something told me to inbox her. I asked her what made her tag me and her response was, "God put it on my heart to tag you." That was my sign and I never dropped another tear after that. That was all the validation that I needed.

Signs of Emotional Abuse

- Jealousy of your relationships with others.
- Threatening to hurt themselves because of you.
- Using guilt/compassion to control you.
- "Gaslighting" Rewriting events to convince you they happened a certain way.
- Blaming you for their actions.
- Your boundaries don't matter.
- Their needs are the only ones that matter.
- Blaming you for things in their life going wrong.
- Shaming you into not talking about it.
- No doesn't mean no.
- They "love bomb" you and then mistreat you.
- Nothing you say or do is good enough.
- Humiliating and berating you.
- Everything is one extreme or the other.
- Constant unfounded accusations of mistrust.

November 2021

We started packing and I told him to not touch any of my belongings because I was getting rid of a lot of items. In actuality, I was packing what was going to my new apartment and what was going to the storage. During my planning, I rented two storage units, one he knew about but the other, he didn't. I marked my boxes with special marking so the people who were helping me would know what boxes went where. As the days went on, I was setting up my new apartment and he had no clue. I could finally see the light at the end of the tunnel. I knew it would be over soon. There was no arguing or disagreeing. At that point I didn't give two shits it was a whole lot of "ok, no problem, anything you want" going on. I had absolutely no reason to debate anything with him because I knew I was outta there. I planned the hell out of that move. I applied for three credit cards in his name. I gave him two and kept one just in case he damaged the house prior to leaving. You do not know what a person will do when they feel like they are losing control over what's "theirs." Remember, narcissists don't view you as a person, they view you as their property and no one wants to lose what they deem as theirs so move accordingly……

He was not working, he was on Workers Comp when we moved to Houston. In April 2021, his attorney told him that he could start looking for work since his case was coming to an end but he still sat on his ass and that was the final straw. Once I saw that he had no drive or motivation to go get a job and that he was clearly okay with me handling everything, I knew that it was time for me go.

He did not have any family in Houston; he was blessed that I am not a cold-hearted person but, trust me, if we were still in California, I would have left his ass with nothing. But, I wanted him to at least still be able to take his things and get back to California. I made up my mind to leave him $2,000 in cash, which was half of the money we made from selling the items in the house. I left all of his and his children's important documents along with our wedding pictures and his car and house keys. I left everything in the middle of the floor in the kitchen on top of a box.

December 1, 2021
My Freedom Day!

On the morning of 12/1/21, my daughter Azhane and I got up and picked up the U-Haul truck and parked it around the corner. She was in town for Thanksgiving and had stayed to help me move. We were going on with our day as normal. 2:40 p.m. rolled around and I dropped him off at the Dentist office. I gave him a kiss, told him I loved him and drove off. I did not see him again...The absolute best day of my life!

By the time I got back home, my daughter had the U-Haul backed up to the house and she was throwing shit in. My God-Sister Qiana pulled up and shortly after my good friend Anita pulled up. We were hauling ass to get my stuff out and we did it in under 2 hours. I can remember a point that I just stopped, I burst out into tears, not because I was sad but because I was having to leave in this manner. The tears lasted maybe 30 seconds, and I was right back into action. We were wrapping up and he called and said he was almost done. I told him that I had to drop my daughter off to the airport so she could go home and I would send a Uber to pick him up and he said it was fine, he would walk. His Dentist appointment was maybe a 15 min walk from our house so I said okay. We closed the U-Haul door and drove off. That was one of the best days of my life. I WAS FUCKING FREE!!

And now for the aftermath

He got home and didn't notice that half of the remaining items were gone. The only thing he noticed was that my truck key was no longer on his key ring. Now mind you, the keys were sitting on top of a box in the kitchen with cash, credit cards, pictures and documents, but the FIRST thing he noticed that was that MY key was gone. He immediately texted me to ask why my key was no longer on his key ring. That's when I sent him the pre-populated text message that I had saved for this very moment, you see I knew I had to go no contact...

I told you I wanted a divorce and you didn't listen, you never did, which is why we are here. You have until December 8th, at 5pm to vacate 2818 Durham Chase Katy, TX 77449. I left the key to the storage on the counter, you can go in there and take whatever you want. I don't want any of it, you can have it all. The storage is only there for 1 month unless you transfer it into your name. I have 1 credit card in your name that has a balance of $2,000 and you have the Spirit Airline credit card and I left another card for you that has $1,500 on it. I am leaving you $2,000 which includes the rest of your money that I had, your $600 tax return and $1000 from the items we sold. Please leave the house in the same condition that it was in when we moved in. I took videos before I left. Please don't try to find me. I will only talk to your mom. Once I have the landlord confirm that you did not destroy the house, I will mail your credit card with any remaining balance that is on it unless you do damage, then it will be paid for with that card and the remaining balance will be mailed certified mail to your mother's address. If you do not want them sent there please tell her. I will give Fred your gun and I am not giving you either 9mm gun that is in my name for my safety against you and hopefully to keep you from harming yourself. You have until Dec 5th to take your phone out of my name before I disconnect it. I will allow you to remain on my benefits until you get a job or the divorce is final but only if you pay your monthly premiums and copay on the 1st of the month, the first time you miss a payment, you will be dropped and I am dropping you off of my car insurance as of December 1.

You can put whatever you need to put in that storage until you figure out where you will go. The best thing for you to do is have your son fly out here and you get a U-Haul and drive everything back to Cali and get your sons, they need you. You have credit with Southwest totaling $346.98. The confirmation numbers for the credit are (3JPSUT) (46V747). Fly your son here with that. I left you everything you need to continue to run Ucci Cute and Saucy I do not want any parts of it. I left the Mac Computer, heat press, Cricut, vinyl and clothes. I took the t-shirts and sublimation Hoodies. Please remove your car from the house. I gave you my all and that still was not enough. You need help, you are a Narcissist. I will have my Attorney reach out to you. I wish you nothing but the best in life.

I am leaving you $2,000 in cash.
Capital one Card ending in 2951 $1,653.
Mission lane Card ending in 6979 $2,000 I have.
Spirit airlines Card ending in 2383 $1,874.
I left your credit cards, COVID card and your children's birth certificates in an envelope.

And I blocked him……

After a few days I unblocked him because I had to talk to him about the house but I would only talk through text. He tried his best to get me back. He sent flowers to my UPS box and candles. Now he knew I loved candles but he would always complain when I lit them; he knew I loved flowers and would withhold them from me and would only give them to me on occasions that he deemed special or right after we got into a big argument. He said he thought it was fake to buy me flowers "just because" even though he knew I loved flowers but, that's what narcissists do, they withhold the very thing they know you love as a form of punishment. He tried to go back to the love bombing stage again and he thought by sending me gifts that it would change my mind, no sir, FUCK YOU! I would never go back, he could kiss my ass and kick rocks!!!! I WAS DONE!!!

January 18, 2022

January 18, 2022, I filed for divorce. I remember it as if it was yesterday. I walked into my Attorney's office, we went over the paperwork, and I signed off on everything. The divorce was in motion but I had to pay $500 to file and I sure as hell wasn't coming out of my pocket so, what did I do? Yep, you guessed it. I texted him and asked him if he had any money he could spare, and said that I needed $500. Before I could hit send good, he sent it and I sent it right to my Attorney. I had given up enough and I was not coming up off of anything else! She looked at me when I told her what I had done and all she could do was laugh. She thanked me and I left.

He tried a last-ditch effort to get me back. One of his friends was dealing with a similar situation and thought it would be helpful to gift him with four therapy sessions. I agreed to attend. It was over Zoom, so I said, "Sure why not," but I definitely had other plans. I was ready when the Zoom started. I was emotionless. I hadn't seen him since the day I left. The Zoom started with the husband-and-wife therapists. They started with me. The very first question they asked was "What are you looking to get out of this therapy session?" I cleared my throat and said "I AM NOT LOOKING TO GET ANYTHING OUT OF THIS SESSION, I NEED YOU ALL TO HELP HIM UNDERSTAND THAT THIS MARRAIGE IS OVER!!!!" His water works started immediately and I was not moved, I WAS DONE!!! ZOOM OVER!

March 17, 2022

March 17th was operation have his ass served day. A few days prior, I had reached out to him to see if he would be in Houston, and if so, if we could meet up so I could give him the rest of his stuff. Of course he said yes, he hadn't seen me since 12/1/21, so I knew he would be willing to meet. I told him to meet me at a local pizza place that he liked but little did he know, he would be meeting my process server. The time was set for 6:00 p.m. For the first time in years, he was on time and so was my process server. The process server noticed that he wasn't getting out of his car and that's when it dawned on us that he was waiting for me to pull up so I had to think quick. I texted him and told him to go inside and order, that I was coming down the street and he went for it. As soon as he got out and closed his car door the server handed him the papers.

You see in Texas, you have 30 days after the 1st Monday in which you are served to contest the divorce but he had someone in his ear telling him that if he didn't sign that would hold it up. Yes that works in California but not in Texas, baby if you do not respond within 30 days, the divorce automatically goes through.

April 13, 2022

Our Court date came and he did not appear, so the divorce was pushed through. It was the fastest divorce ever! It only took 2 months. Luckily, we shared no children or property together.

I was finally totally FUCKING FREE!!!!!!

Thankfully, I did not skip a beat in life. I kept going as if nothing ever happened. I am so thankful that I was able to move the way I did. There are so many women who cannot leave, whether it is due to financial reasons, or just not being mentally ready to leave. Having children with a narcissist will make it ten times worse when you attempt to leave. I thank God every day for keeping me from making that mistake of giving him a child. Truth be told, him and the baby would have gotten left, lol.

Knowing what I know, there were definitely some red flags from the beginning but, if you have never been taught about red flags, then you will not know what to look for. Remember **"Red flags do not look or feel like red flags when they feel like home."**

During the process of me leaving, I realized that there were so many women going through the same thing as me but we all were suffering in silence in fear of embarrassment and judgement. This led me to create my Facebook group "The Circle." The Women's Healing Circle provides a space for Women to come together in a supportive environment that is culturally safe, to talk and heal together. Since my divorce, I have become a Certified Healing Life Coach, and started a Nonprofit 501(c)3 called "The Healing Circle." Since sharing my story publicly, I have helped so many women through their own struggles of dealing with a narcissist. I was shocked to learn of the high number of women and men that have fallen victim to a Narcissist.

Know there is light at the end of the tunnel and know that you are not crazy. When dealing with a narcissist, they will have you really thinking that you are losing your mind. Always move in silence and don't let them know what your plans are. If you plan on leaving, only you know what you are up against and the type of person that you are dealing with so move accordingly and safety first.

Chapter 2
Running Nowhere!
Kam

He was my male best friend, my partner in crime. We met each other at the tender age of 15. Immediately, we became cool. Throughout our years of growing up, we stayed connected. There would be times that we didn't see each other, but when we did, baby it was always laughter, and a bunch of fun! The 'lust' we shared was everything. There was nothing he wouldn't do for me.

Once we were grown grown, I saw it all! The good, bad and the ugly! Every part of him was mine. Including the parts that I did not want.

Hell, I didn't see any of it coming. I was blinded by the trips, gifts, flowers, and dinners. You name it, he gave it to me. Eventually, though I felt that he wanted to control me. And he did! He even put sugar in my tank! It got worse and I felt like I was running all the time.

Running...Now we're under the same roof.
 Running...Now he's moved out.
Running...we're still fucking.
Running...calling everybody, snotting and crying.
Running...damn, bitch are you becoming a NARC, is what I had to ask myself.

Running... on my knees crying out to the Lord.
During this time of my life, I truly thank God for Sarah Jakes Robert's. Whewww, chile listen!

No matter what, we have to keep pushing. Everybody doesn't need to know your business. Find you a safe spot and stick with it. There's more to my story. But I have kept running Nowhere! I'm still fighting this demon. Spirits are real. While going through, look in the mirror and remind yourself, that you are beautiful and loved by you.

Passing a hug and sending love.

Chapter 3
Disguised Devil
Anna Hayter

We met when we were around 16/17 years old. I was warned by my family to stay away from his family. He was the kind of "man" that had me feeling like I was the only woman in the world. I got pregnant at 17 and I had our son at 18. At the time, he was a provider and made sure we were always good. He definitely had me feeling like I had the prize. Once we moved into our own place, his mother and stepfather moved in with us. The first signs of abuse came after our son was born. When he would get mad, he would chuck his Jordan's at me with full power.

From there, there was rape, choking, a marriage to another woman, me taking him back over and over, until he decided to start dating a 17-year-old; he was 29. He abused me in front of our kids and raped me in front of our daughter while I was pregnant with our 3rd child in the car behind a grocery store. So much more has happened and I can say I've stayed away from him since 2009! I dealt with so much for 13 years on and off.

Chapter 4
Pastor NO NO
Anonymous

I survived! It's crazy because I had never heard of a narcissist until I met and married one. I've dated a few but nothing like this. One day I was playing around on social media. I came across a guy and we joked back and forth and then the inbox came. He gave me his number and later asked me out. Our first date was nice. You can always tell from the first date if you want to go on another one. He was the perfect gentleman, opening doors and helping me all the time, talking about how much he prayed for a woman like me to marry one day. He said I was perfect and he saw me in his dreams before he met me. By our 5th or 6th date, he was already discussing commitment and marriage. He was volunteering, helping with the kids and the household. We had been dating for 5 months, and he asked me if I would marry him in the future. I said yes, I would if we fell in love and we both wanted too. He was very serious and persistent. My birthday was approaching, and my friends made plans to take me out to eat. The night was so unexpected. He was acting weird but I thought it was because I didn't include him, but he acted like he was happy that I was going out to enjoy myself.

So I went out and we were having a real good time. He texted me out of the blue to ask what restaurant I was at so he could drop off my present. The fact that he thought of me enough to do that made me feel special. We knew he was coming so we all walked out after dinner; he pulled up and walked over to me in front of my friend and got on his knees and there it was, a promise ring and a card, promising to be my man and later my husband.

This was my first time feeling this special in a long time. Everyone around was staring and tearing up, they were so happy for me. We decided to wait a year before marriage, that was the plan, at least I thought. He forced me to marry him early in a small private wedding because he didn't want anyone in our business, so he said. When you're being love bombed, you overlook the signs of control, it starts with isolation. I agreed and we got married. My life changed and after the first year of marriage, I was a slave, a prisoner in my own home. I was also labeled the bad guy. I couldn't spend time with friends or family and was constantly being accused of cheating to justify his behavior.

I became a shell, living under his surveillance 24/7, it was a nightmare. I had been planning the day I was going to leave for months because the first time I expressed it, he got violent, so I knew I needed a plan B. I left him while he was at work. I took my son and my dog and never looked back. It was the best decision I could have made. The trauma from that marriage has caused anxiety and PTSD and the fear of getting into another relationship, but as time heals, the wounds will too.

Chapter 5
The OnlyFans Pastor
Khalilah Anderson

Another day, another dollar. It was the morning of Wednesday, January 28, 2021, and I had an important meeting at work. I was the lead for HR in my department and I had to terminate an employee for practicing medicine without a license. This meeting was going to be a lot of back and forth, but the outcome would remain unchanged. Rehearsing the meeting in my mind, I headed to the garage, dressed in a black pants suit, work appropriate heels, freshly twisted locs, and light makeup to highlight my brown skin. I got into my gray Volvo S90, started it and prepared to back out of the garage. My daughter, Trenyce, opened the door to the garage. She still had her bonnet on, covering her fresh 20-inch bundles, and her pajamas. Our eyes locked and I noticed a look of complete distress all over her 5ft petite frame. It was a look that I had never seen from her before. I rolled down my window and asked, "What's Up?" "You're going to work?" she asked in a panic. I responded, "Yes, it's my day in the office." She quickly answered, "I need to talk to you." I calmly replied, "Ok." I had no clue what she wanted to tell me but whatever it was, I knew it was going to be terrible. I took a deep breath and told her that I had to go into work to take care of a meeting but as soon as the meeting ended, I would leave to come home early.

She seemed really anxious but accepted my response and stepped back into the house. I pulled my car out of the garage and tried to brace myself for whatever was coming. I did not have a clue as to what it could be but the knots in my stomach let me know that it was going to be something really bad. I would have to deal with whatever it was later. I pushed the thoughts of what could be from my mind and started rehearsing my notes for the meeting.

Two nights before, I was lounging in the loft with my husband, Pastor, Civil Rights Leader, President of a large Baptist Ministers association, and political advisor, Kelv. We were watching a movie when Trenyce came and asked me if her childhood friend, Diamond, could spend the night at our house. They were going to Las Vegas for a friend trip and needed to run some errands together prior to the trip; it was more convenient for Diamond to spend the night at our house rather than Trenyce making multiple trips to drop her off and pick her up.

I'd known Diamond almost her entire life, as I did most of Trenyce's friends. She was about 23 years old at the time and had spent the night with us regularly over the years without issue. When Trenyce was growing up, my house had always been the house where the girls could spend the night, I considered it a safe space. We lived alone and I felt better knowing the girls were with me, in a house without any boys or men around to make them feel uncomfortable.

For the first time, Trenyce asking if a friend could sleepover sounded strange. I hesitated to respond. I turned to Kelv for approval. "Babe, do you mind if Trenyce's friend spends the night tomorrow?" He knew who Diamond was and responded, "No, it's fine," so I gave Trenyce the green light but, in that moment, my stomach turned. I felt that something was off. I quickly silenced the voice in my head believing that it was just nerves. Trenyce had never had a friend sleepover with a man in the house and for some reason alarms were going off like crazy. "You're tripping, that's your husband," I said to myself. Somehow, my body was signaling to me that my life would never be the same after that weekend.

See, Diamond had an OnlyFans page. For those who don't know, OnlyFans is an internet content subscription service, used for pornography to help subscribers enact their deep sexual fantasies. The site allows for erotic pictures, videos, direct messages, and the ability to leave "tips" for your favorites. I knew about Diamond's page but how would Kelv know? He couldn't, right? Diamond was family and had always been respectful. She was like a daughter to me. Nothing could possibly go wrong, I thought, trying to convince myself.

I wrapped up the meeting at work, went to my office, grabbed my things and headed to my car. I had just terminated the employee against multiple objections from him and his union rep. That was done so I tried to prepare mentally to face the issue that was waiting for me at home. I told myself that whatever she said to me, I would remain calm. I had no clue what it could be. Was she pregnant? I doubted it but could not come up with anything solid. I just knew it was not going to be good so I just kept telling myself to listen and understand no matter what.

What was a 30-minute drive home seemed to take about 10 minutes. I turned into the driveway and hit the button to open the garage. Trenyce and Diamond appeared. They walked quickly to my car and got in. Trenyce sat in the front seat and Diamond got into the back. It was obvious that whatever they had to tell me, they did not want to talk about in the house. That's definitely a red flag, I thought. Without saying anything, I put the car in reverse, backed out of the driveway and drove away from the house. "I have something really bad to tell you about Kelv," Trenyce started. "Ok," I replied. She began telling me that Kelv had been on Diamond's OnlyFans page sending her messages and leaving her tips anonymously for months. He did not have a profile picture on his page and was going by the name Ken. Over a period of months, starting before we got married, Kelv had been sending Diamond messages in an attempt to meet up with her and eventually have sex with her.

Kelv wanted so bad to have sex with his soon-to-be stepdaughter's friend. He was relentless in his pursuit of her, constantly asking to meet up. Diamond consistently told him that she did not meet up with fans, she provided online services only. Kelv kept insisting that he wanted a physical relationship with her and that he wanted to see her. He promised to spoil her and told her that he was an older man with lots of cash, so money would not be a problem. He wanted to get her into a hotel room by any means. He sent tips and messages frequently to keep her attention. In his twisted mind, Kelv thought that Diamond's hesitance to meet up with him may have been related to COVID so he sent a message saying that she did not have to worry about them getting a hotel room because he had already had COVID. Her response was unchanged.

Kelv's mind was clearly all over the place and he was desperate to maintain communication with her. He started telling Diamond that he knew some of her friends. He would never say who but would drop subtle hints and started a guessing game, with hints here and there, followed by, do you know who I am now? He then told Diamond that he had met her before. What he left out was that he had met her at our wedding, in our home, where she was working, as the photographer. You read that correctly, Diamond took our wedding photos in our home on our wedding day. As we were taking vows, he was likely lusting over her and the images he had seen of her on Only Fans.

Diamond never joined in the game; not only did she show no interest in the game, she was actually annoyed by it. See Diamond was on OnlyFans for funds, which most people are. It's a job, a means to make money. The purpose is to engage fans and get tips, but meeting up and playing mind games was not part of it. The more that Diamond displayed a lack of interest in knowing who he was, the more he fantasized about revealing himself to her. Kelv was really sick. He told Diamond that he wanted her to know who he was, but insisted that if he revealed himself, she had to keep his identity confidential. Kelv repeatedly asked to meet up with her and started sharing his schedule, I guess in hopes that one day she would say she was available too and agree to meet up with him. Kelv started going further and further, going so far as to tell Diamond that he lived in Ontario. Another hint. Diamond replied by saying that it should be obvious that she was not interested in meeting up and that she was never going to give in to his "guess who" game. Kelv still did not get it and would not take no for an answer. He asked for her CashApp and then told her that when she received the money, she would know who he was, but still he asked her to guess his identity again first. He told her to just guess, and he would send the CashApp even if her guess was incorrect. The idea of her possibly guessing his identity turned him on.

The night when I asked Kelv if Diamond could spend the night in our home, unbeknownst to me, he was very excited and immediately sent her a message on OnlyFans. We had recently seen Diamond at a local casino. I said hello to her and the friend that she was with, but Kelv kept walking. I thought it was strange that he did not speak to her considering he had met her before and she had been in our home, but I brushed it off. Your body always gives you signs. Anyway, in the message that Kelv sent to Diamond, he said, "I saw you recently and I hear I'm going to see you again. Do you know who I am?"

At this point, Diamond had had enough. She asked him where he had seen her recently and then told him she really didn't give a fuck. Kelv backed down and told her that he would give her some cash soon. Up until that point, Trenyce had done most of the talking. Diamond jumped in and began telling me that it was always a sick and twisted game but that he had lost his mind when she got in our home, he could no longer control himself. While she was in our guest room and while he was possibly laying next to me, he sent Diamond a message that said, "I want a video tonight." Diamond responded that she was at a friend's house in a guest room and may not be able to send the video. Kelv's response was, "You can! Be loud." Then he told her to go outside of the guest room and look for a black book on the desk and open the cover. He said, "Have a good trip. Guess you know now."

Diamond immediately went to Trenyce and said somebody in this house has been sending me messages. She showed Trenyce the thread and she was shocked. At first, Trenyce thought it was his teenage son. It had to be, right? It couldn't be Kelv. But then she saw the emojis. The black raised fist and the heart.

Kelv used that emoji combination all of the time. Trenyce's stomach turned and they knew they had to tell me. I listened intently, I never interrupted and I never doubted. I knew it was true and I knew how heavy the burden was of them telling me. The first words out of my mouth were "I'm so sorry. I'm sorry this happened to you at my house and I'm sorry you all had to experience this. Thank you for telling me." Then I wanted to know if Diamond still had the messages. She did. I asked her to send them to me and she did. Next, I told them to get their things. I was sending them to a hotel. They were not scheduled to leave for their trip to Vegas until the next day and I could not let them spend another night in that house under the same roof with him. I needed them to feel safe and there was no way that would happen under those circumstances. As I was on my phone looking for hotel accommodations, they were both crying out loud. Their eyes were full of sadness, fear, and hurt for me. My daughter was hurt and ashamed. She was ashamed that her mom's husband had tried to sleep with her friend.

They did not want to leave me in the house with him. I assume they were afraid of what might happen when they left. However, I was never afraid. God had clothed me in peace. At that moment, I was not even angry. I assured them that none of it was their fault, that I was fine, and that they should still go to Las Vegas for the weekend.

As they gathered their things to go to the hotel, I went upstairs into the loft, where I knew he would be, tapping away on the controller to his PS5, playing an NBA video game. "You gave Trenyce's friend some money," it was more of a question than a statement. Keeping his eyes on the television screen, he replied, "No." "So you didn't give her any money," I questioned. He said, "No, I haven't said anything to that girl since she came here." "Ok" I said and turned and walked downstairs to Trenyce's room where they were packing their things for the night and weekend for their trip.

I knew the truth, but I wanted him to have to face Diamond after what he did to her. I asked her if she felt comfortable confronting him and she immediately said yes. I told them that he denied giving her any money at all. Furious, Diamond went into her purse and pulled out three crisp $100 dollar bills. There was fire in her eyes and I knew she was ready. We went back upstairs; he had left the loft and retreated behind closed doors into our bedroom.

I opened the door to find him whispering on the phone. Diamond jumped right in, holding her hand out, showing him the $300 cash, and fiercely saying "You gave this to me."

Kelv looked shocked and terrified by her boldness. I don't think he ever expected her to confront him or even say anything. He viewed her as young and vulnerable. Kelv thought that Diamond needed the money and for a few dollars she would stay quiet, betray us, and sell herself to him. Kelv never guessed that Diamond was courageous, loyal, and a young lady with morals and values. She was better than him but he thought otherwise, and now he had to face both of us. Kelv was like a deer in headlights. He said, "I'm not talking to anybody." Still holding her hand out with the money in it, Diamond repeated herself, "You gave me this money!" Shaking his head, actually, his whole body may have been shaking, he replied again, "I'm not talking to anybody." He was still on the phone and using that as an excuse to keep from having a real conversation. I grabbed Diamond by the hand and we walked out of the room together. That was enough.

As we were walking away, Trenyce met us in the hallway, she was crying uncontrollably. Diamond hugged her and began crying too. I held them both as they cried in my arms. Kelv's teenage son had been in his bedroom the whole time. He opened the door and saw us. He had a look of confusion on his face but quickly closed the door and went back into his room. They started telling me that they did not want to leave me in the house with him. He was evil and they were afraid of what he may do to me. I assured them again that I was fine and told them that they were young and deserved to go have fun and enjoy themselves.

They had been planning this trip for months now. I let them know that I could handle myself and that I had no fear at all. I had already made the hotel reservation and given Trenyce the money to pay for the room. I gave them the hotel information, told them to go and to let me know once they were checked in and settled. Against their wishes, they loaded their bags into Trenyce's car and drove away, not knowing what would happen next.

I knew the truth. There was nothing to discuss or argue about. My husband had tried to sleep with Trenyce's friend, Diamond, I saw her as a daughter. She took our wedding photos. I felt like I must have been dreaming. This man had gone above and beyond to show me how much he loved me. I did not know it yet, but I had married a narcissist, who had love bombed me and manipulated me from the beginning. This stunt with Diamond was carried out to fulfill his freaky, perverted desires but it was also an attempt to break me and isolate me from my daughter while destroying other lifelong relationships in the process. If successful, his plan would have left me at his mercy and on a path of destruction. It did not work and I was faced with the truth. He was never sorry. Not only did he fail to take accountability for his actions or show remorse, he also gaslit and blamed me for bringing Diamond into our home. Everything that happened was mine and my daughter's fault. In fact, Trenyce had set him up because, according to him, she never liked him. He spoke all of these things matter-of-factly. Even people who knew the truth almost believed him. He was a master manipulator and liar. I started to realize that Kelv was evil and it was just beginning...

Chapter 6
The Man Who Wore A Mask
Nailah Dixon

I'll never forget the day. It was July 4, 2008. I stepped out to enjoy the night with a close friend. We headed to San Francisco, all smiles and giggles, ready to enjoy the night.

I knew I was cute. I stepped off of the train ready to party and was soon disappointed because the club we went to was dead. So my friend and I left. As we walked back towards downtown, we heard a man's voice, "Oh, ya'll aren't coming to party with us?" I replied "Oh nah, we are headed home now!" As I turned around to see who I was speaking to, I saw him (let's just call him Country). He was not so tall, and bigger than I liked, but he had an accent and I'm a sucker for a nice southern accent. We exchanged pleasantries and then phone numbers and I trotted happily towards the nearest train station to head home.

A few days had passed, and I decided to reach out and say hello. I didn't quite remember what he looked liked, but I was thinking "What's the harm?! I'm not gonna marry him..." We talked, and the conversation was amazing. I mean, this man said all of the right things. He seemed respectful, family oriented, and constantly reminded me of how beautiful I was. Eventually, we agreed to go out. And that's when I should have noticed the red flags. First off, he spoke as if he had a car, and I ended up driving on our 1st date. After that, the excuses just seemed to overflow.

About a month into dating, he found out that his cousin hadn't been paying rent. And you guessed it, he needed a place to stay. I obliged. Things just got worse as time progressed. It's like God was showing me all of the signs and I just kept ignoring them. Even my mom said I should have been a bit more cautious.

So I blinked twice and we were 2 months in. Things were going good until I got laid off and on the very same day, I found out I was pregnant. SMH. He was excited, and it eased my fears about whether I should proceed with the pregnancy or not. He went out and immediately got a 2nd job and I was able to chill until I found a retail job to help make ends meet. It wasn't until the baby was born that the fuckery really began. Picture this: We were sitting on the couch and he started crying. I was looking at him like "Wtf?" He said, "I gotta tell you something but you're going to judge me." "I won't. I love you," I replied. "You will because you already said it before," (cries hysterically) "I'm a registered sex offender and I was set up by my mothers husband!" That took a minute to digest.

We talked about it and then I met his family. All of their stories seemed to be in alignment so I stayed and tried to fix Country and love him through his mess. Instead, this is where I should have let him go.

Our son was born and when he was 5 weeks old, I was going out of town to my family reunion. There was nothing going on at home that would make me believe that Country was doing anything other than being the amazing man and father that he portrayed himself to be. As I prepared to leave, he wished me well, and I took my then 5 year-old and our 5 week old with me for the weekend.

Communication was fine while I was gone, Country and I talked and laughed and he checked on the baby. It wasn't until I was on my way back that I felt something was off. He kept asking me "How far out are you?" "Do you know when you'll be back?" I thought to myself, I wonder why he keeps asking me this… but I just shrugged it off and focused on the drive back home.

The kids and I got home pretty late, and Country was at "work." He always chose to work night jobs and always worked 7 days a week. How convenient, right? The next day, we were at home with the kids and the baby was fussy. I asked him to hold the baby while I went to grab something. He was so into his phone that he almost dropped the baby. He turned and looked at me wide eyed and replied "Huh?" It was in that moment that I knew I had to check his phone. Now keep in mind we were in a beautiful place and in love more than ever, or so I thought. We went to sleep that night, and I woke up to feed the baby when I saw that he had left his phone out in the open. After tending to the baby, I took his phone into the bathroom and what I saw next caved my chest in.

Her: You gone give your baby mama some of that good good tonight?!
Him: Nah, she's on her period.
Her: I wish I could get some. I'm sure I can taste her when I suck your dick. I don't care.

My blood was boiling. How? Why? I stepped into the bedroom and turned the light on "Who is this bitch and why are you telling her all of my business?" He responded, "Huh? What are you talking about?" I started reading the messages, and he yelled "I'm sorry! (started crying) This is the most freedom I've had in a relationship and I fucked up! You never go through my stuff or question me about anything." I felt bad. Why did I overreact like that, I thought. I mean, he has been through a lot. I forgave him and this is when that hamster wheel started turning...

After that initial encounter, there were so many women that I lost track. But the one I remember was Kim. He loved her. He even eventually talked me into not being friends with him on social media so that our relationship would flourish. What he really did was block me and Kim along with her friend J would comment on his pics, feeding his ego. He loved it. They'd say how handsome he was and how cute the baby was, and he was eating it up. As the days went by, I found out more and more. We would argue and he'd say things like "You can't take my son from me!" "I'll leave and take my son to Texas!" So, I was trying to do all I could to stop him from cheating and to keep my family together.

42

The next big blow out came and I found out that he was still talking to Kim. But plot twist, he was talking to her and her friend! And neither of them were aware. I told them both and I'll never forget what happened next. He came in the kitchen and he was livid. "What the fuck is wrong with you?" SLAP!! He had hit me! I just stood there. I couldn't believe it. He then called his friend Manny and said, "Man come get me! I just slapped the shit out this bitch!" I just stood there in disbelief. My oldest son was in ear shot and had heard everything. I told him to stay put when he called for me. I went to the bathroom to wash my face and shortly after the texts rolled in. He was apologizing, but also blaming me. "I'm sorry for hitting you like that but you told them that. Why?" I thought to myself, that was wrong. I should have just minded my business. I mean he's still paying the bills. And just like that, in a couple of days he was back home like he'd never left.

The drama died down and we were back to normal, laughing and chilling. But little did I know, there was ALWAYS someone in the wings waiting.

The stories were so colorful. He would tell them how he was taking care of me and the kids, how we weren't together but we lived together for the kids. It was just insane. And like clockwork, every time he got caught, he would hit me, cry, and we would start over.

Like the time he met Bella. At the time, I had no idea she was 16. But I later found out she was under age. He would walk or drive my car when I was sleep just to go and see her. I remember I took my car keys because I had had enough, and he wanted to "run to the store." I said no, and an argument ensued. Once it was over, he had taken my keys and put them in the car door outside and then cried about how I couldn't take his only son from him. I thank God nobody stole my car. It was almost like he knew I wanted to leave but he wasn't quite sure when his last day of playing these games would be.

As the years progressed, no matter how bad I wanted him to, Country just wouldn't change. I mean I went so far as to make a fake Facebook account. I would talk to him as if I were another woman. I had him eating from the palm of my hand, but at home he wouldn't bite. It's like he loved the attention from being whoever he wanted to be online, but he hated the attention from me. I would see him liking certain food recipes online and cook them for him at home; he never ate them. It got so bad at one point I asked him why he wouldn't just leave me. He could never give an answer. I now know this is what narcissists do. I realized he would rather me be miserable with him than happy with someone else. It's like he knew I was a good woman, and he wanted that and all of the benefits of being with me.

As the years went on, I got tired. So I found the husband of his main side chick. I created a text free account and started talking to him. I planned to do the most disgusting and vile things to him and come home and kiss Country in the mouth. Just as I was about to strike, the other woman found out and told him. He went through my phone and deleted and blocked the other man. I was furious. "You can have your fun, why can't I!" About 1-2 months later, he proposed. I foolishly obliged, and we were married a year later. He was on hie best behavior or so I thought.

We weren't even 2 years into our marriage when things went completely down hill. Country and I were simply existing. He was still abusing me and my children, cheating and being a complete asshole. I had began to feel overcome with resentment. I was tired. "Why did I marry him?" I asked myself. He never complimented me and didn't want me dressing up. He never took me out and never spent time with me. This was the beginning of the end. I had an escape plan and hiding place for me and the kids should he ever beat me or them again. They knew what to do, where to go, who to call and what to wait for. "What kind of life is this," I used to ask myself. But silly me, still wasn't ready.

I started traveling and going out without him. And when a good friend of mine found her now husband, I started hanging out with them more and taking the kids with me. He hated that. He hated the fact that he couldn't make me miserable anymore. So one day he started an argument. And he said "If you were more focused on your own relationship instead of your friends we would be cool!" I replied "I like him for her! He's funny and cool to hang with and you would know that if you spoke when he came around!" BAM! He knocked my cup out of my hand as I sat on the bed sipping my coffee. He stood over me holding me with one hand and holding his fist over me with the other. Yelling, he said "So you think he's funny? Huh?" I saw the rage in his eyes. Our daughter was asleep next to me, and she woke up. She stood in the bed trembling and paralyzed with fear. He demanded she get out, and I told her to stay. I held my baby and he started to throw things across the room. I believe she saved my life. He was definitely going to beat me bad that day. And that was it. I said "YOU GOTTA GO!" He yelled, "Oh so you want me out?" "Yes," I replied.

After the storm, I got up and began to clean my room. While this whole ordeal had been going on, my oldest son and his brother were in the shower in their bathroom hiding and recording audio waiting for the code word to call the police. Oh yeah, we had a safety word too. So once the dust settled, I walked to the kitchen and guess what was he doing? CRYING!

He was talking to his Mother, playing the victim. He claimed I was abusing him and that he may need to come back home to Texas because there was nothing left here for him. I looked at him and shook my head and proceeded to go back to my room. There was no amount of crying, gifts, explaining or anything else that could make me stay. I was done. It was finally over.

I gave him until the 1st of the month to leave. And it couldn't come fast enough. During the waiting period, he only dealt with our daughter. He kept my other kids and I on ice. We had grown used to it. He would go months without speaking or dealing with me and the boys. He left a few weeks later and my house seemed lighter. The rooms were brighter, my children and I were more harmonious and we began our healing journey. It wasn't easy going from 2 incomes to 1, but I was determined. He used to try and guilt me by coming to drop money off for the kids ($40 here and there) or say he wanted to come see them just to lay on my couch and sleep and monitor what I had going on. I put an end to that, and his presence slowly diminished.

He has since abandoned our children and got the car that we purchased in my name repossessed, I guess as a way to hurt me. But it's okay, my children and I are healthy and have started over. All of Country's attempts to come back have failed and I am now remarried. Meanwhile, he's somewhere telling people how I wronged him. But I don't care! I am free. I walked away with my peace and dignity! I survived my narc.

Understanding Narcissism

Narcissism is a complex personality trait or disorder that can manifest in various ways, ranging from a healthy level of self-esteem to an extreme form characterized by an inflated sense of self-importance, a deep need for excessive attention, and a lack of empathy for others. It is often discussed in two key contexts: as a general personality trait and as Narcissistic Personality Disorder (NPD), a more severe and diagnosable condition.

Key Characteristics of Narcissism
1. Inflated Sense of Self-Importance: Narcissists often believe they are superior to others, deserving of special treatment and admiration.
2. Need for Excessive Attention and Admiration: They often crave validation and compliments to maintain their inflated self-view.
3. Lack of Empathy: Narcissists struggle to understand or care about the feelings and needs of others, making their relationships often one-sided.
4. Entitlement: They believe that they are inherently deserving of privileges or recognition without regard to merit or effort.
5. Exploitative Behavior: Narcissists may take advantage of others to achieve their own goals, showing little concern for the consequences on others.
6. Envy: They may feel envious of others' success and simultaneously believe that others envy them.

Narcissistic Personality Disorder (NPD)

NPD is a more extreme form of narcissism, recognized as a mental health condition. Individuals with NPD exhibit the above traits in ways that significantly impair their ability to function in daily life, maintain relationships, or succeed in work and social settings.

Types of Narcissism

- Grandiose Narcissism: This is the classic type often associated with arrogance, dominance, and a sense of superiority.
- Vulnerable Narcissism: This type involves hypersensitivity to criticism, insecurity, and deep emotional wounds that are often masked by defensive behaviors.

Origins and Causes

- Narcissism can develop from a combination of genetic, environmental, and psychological factors. Some potential causes include:
  - Childhood experiences: Overindulgent or neglectful parenting can contribute to narcissistic traits.
  - Genetics: There may be a genetic predisposition toward narcissism.
  - Cultural influences: Societies or environments that promote competition, individualism, or superficial success may foster narcissistic behaviors.

Effects on Relationships

Narcissists often struggle in personal relationships because their self-centered behavior can lead to emotional manipulation, control, and a lack of true connection with others. They may initially appear charming or charismatic but eventually drain those around them through their constant need for admiration and lack of emotional support.

Healthy Narcissism vs. Pathological Narcissism

Some level of narcissism is considered normal and healthy, as it can help with confidence and ambition. However, when narcissistic traits dominate a person's personality and harm their relationships or functioning, it crosses into the realm of pathological narcissism, such as NPD.

Understanding narcissism involves recognizing its spectrum, from beneficial self-confidence to its harmful extremes. It is essential to differentiate between healthy self-esteem and the destructive patterns that characterize severe narcissistic behaviors.

Being in a relationship with a narcissist can have significant emotional, psychological, and even physical consequences. Narcissistic relationships often involve manipulation, lack of empathy, and an imbalance of power, which can make them toxic and damaging to the non-narcissistic partner. Here's an in-depth look at the impacts of such relationships:

1. Emotional Manipulation and Gaslighting

Narcissists often manipulate their partners to maintain control and superiority. One of the most common tactics is gaslighting, where the narcissist makes their partner doubt their reality or perception. This can lead the victim to feel confused, anxious, and question their own judgment.

Examples of Gaslighting:

- Denying things they said or did, even when proven otherwise.
- Minimizing the partner's feelings, telling them they're "too sensitive" or "overreacting."
- Twisting facts to make the partner feel responsible for issues in the relationship.

2. Loss of Identity and Self-Esteem

Narcissists tend to dominate relationships, making it all about their needs and desires. Over time, the partner of a narcissist may begin to lose their sense of self as they constantly cater to the narcissist's demands.

Effects on Self-Esteem:

- Constant criticism, belittling, or devaluation from a narcissistic partner can erode the self-esteem of their partner.
- The partner may feel they are never "good enough" for the narcissist, which can lead to a persistent feeling of inadequacy and self-doubt.

Loss of Personal Identity:

- Narcissists often demand that their partners conform to their preferences, desires, and expectations, leaving little room for the partner to express their own individuality.

3. Chronic Stress and Anxiety

Being in a narcissistic relationship can cause chronic emotional stress due to the unpredictable, manipulative, and controlling behavior of the narcissist. The partner is often walking on eggshells, constantly trying to avoid triggering the narcissist's rage or silent treatment.

Physical and Mental Health Impacts:

- o Chronic stress can lead to anxiety, depression, and physical health issues such as headaches, digestive problems, and sleep disorders.
- o The emotional rollercoaster of highs (when the narcissist is charming) and lows (when they are angry or dismissive) can be exhausting, leading to a state of emotional burnout.

4. Isolation

Narcissists often try to isolate their partners from friends, family, or support networks. This isolation serves to increase their control over the relationship and reduce the likelihood that the partner will seek help or perspective from others.

Impact of Isolation:
- o The partner may become dependent on the narcissist for emotional support and validation.
- o Without an external support system, it becomes harder for the partner to recognize the unhealthy dynamics of the relationship.

5. Codependency

Partners of narcissists may develop codependency, where they derive their sense of worth and identity from taking care of the narcissist or constantly seeking their approval. This dynamic often leads the partner to put their own needs last, prioritizing the narcissist's well-being at their own expense.

Signs of Codependency:

- Difficulty setting boundaries with the narcissist.
- Feeling responsible for the narcissist's emotions and happiness.
- Putting aside personal desires, goals, and needs to maintain the relationship.

6. Cycle of Idealization, Devaluation, and Discard

Narcissistic relationships often follow a predictable cycle that can trap their partner in an emotionally destructive pattern:

- **Idealization:** At the beginning of the relationship, the narcissist may shower their partner with affection, compliments, and attention, creating a sense of euphoria and attachment.
- **Devaluation:** Once the narcissist feels secure in the relationship, they often begin to criticize, belittle, and devalue their partner. The attention and admiration fade, replaced by contempt or indifference.

Discard: In some cases, the narcissist may abruptly end the relationship when the partner no longer serves their needs or when they find a new source of admiration. This phase can leave the partner feeling devastated, confused, and abandoned.

7. Impact on Children

If the narcissist and their partner have children, the children can also suffer from emotional neglect or manipulation. Narcissists often view their children as extensions of themselves, expecting them to meet their emotional needs rather than supporting the child's individuality and well-being.

Children of Narcissists:

- They may grow up feeling inadequate or only valued for their accomplishments.
- Some children may adopt narcissistic traits themselves, while others may become highly empathetic, often taking on a caregiver role in the family.

8. Difficulty in Leaving

Due to the manipulative nature of narcissistic relationships, it can be incredibly hard for a partner to leave. Narcissists often use emotional blackmail, guilt-tripping, or threats of abandonment to keep their partner from leaving.

- Trauma Bonding: This psychological phenomenon occurs when the victim becomes emotionally attached to the abuser through intermittent reinforcement of affection and devaluation. The occasional love and affection make the victim hold on, hoping things will get better.

9. Long-Term Psychological Effects

Even after leaving a narcissistic relationship, the partner may experience long-term effects such as:

- Post-Traumatic Stress Disorder (PTSD): Emotional abuse from a narcissist can lead to symptoms of PTSD, including flashbacks, anxiety, and hypervigilance.
- Trust Issues: Having been deceived, manipulated, and devalued, the partner may struggle to trust others in future relationships.
- Self-Blame: Narcissists often convince their partners that the issues in the relationship are their fault, leading to lingering feelings of guilt or self-blame after the relationship ends.

Healing from a Narcissistic Relationship

Recovery from a narcissistic relationship can take time, but it is possible with support, self-care, and professional guidance. Some key steps include:

- Therapy: Seeking therapy, especially from someone familiar with narcissistic abuse, can help individuals rebuild their self-esteem, understand the dynamics they experienced, and heal emotionally.
- Rebuilding Self-Esteem: Focusing on self-care, setting boundaries, and reconnecting with one's identity are crucial in rebuilding confidence and independence.
- Support Networks: Friends, family, and support groups can provide validation, understanding, and emotional support during the healing process.

The impact of narcissistic relationships can be profound, but with awareness and support, it is possible to break free from the toxic cycle and regain emotional well-being.

Recognizing the Signs

Identifying narcissistic behavior can be challenging because narcissists often present themselves as confident, charming, or successful, particularly in the early stages of a relationship. However, over time, certain patterns of behavior can signal narcissism. Here are key traits and behaviors that can help you identify narcissistic tendencies:

1. Grandiose Sense of Self-Importance
- Narcissists believe they are special, unique, or superior to others. They expect others to admire them and may exaggerate their achievements or talents.
- They may speak in a way that suggests their needs or opinions are more important than those of others.

Examples:
- Frequently talking about their successes while downplaying or ignoring the achievements of others.
- Believing they deserve special treatment, even without merit.

2. Constant Need for Admiration and Validation

- Narcissists crave constant attention and praise. They rely on external validation to maintain their self-esteem, and without it, they may become upset, anxious, or angry.
- They often seek out situations or people who will affirm their inflated self-image.

Examples:

- Fishing for compliments or demanding recognition for minor accomplishments.
- Becoming overly upset or offended when not the center of attention.

3. Lack of Empathy

- Narcissists struggle to recognize or care about the feelings and needs of others. They may appear emotionally detached or indifferent when others are hurt or in need of support.
- This lack of empathy makes them prone to manipulating others for their own benefit without feeling guilt or remorse.

Examples:

- Ignoring a friend's emotional distress or belittling their feelings.
- Exploiting someone's vulnerabilities to gain something for themselves.

4. Sense of Entitlement

- Narcissists believe that they deserve special treatment or privileges. They expect others to cater to their needs without question, and they become frustrated when they are not treated as superior.
- They may disregard social rules or expectations because they believe these don't apply to them.

Examples:

- Expecting others to drop everything to attend to their needs.
- Cutting in line or taking advantage of others' generosity without offering gratitude.

5. Exploitative Behavior

- Narcissists often use others to achieve their own goals or desires. They may take advantage of people's kindness or trust without feeling guilty about it.
- Relationships with narcissists are often one-sided, with the narcissist taking more than they give.

Examples:

- Borrowing money or resources without returning them.
- Using someone's skills, influence, or connections for personal gain without offering anything in return.

6. Envy and Belittlement of Others

- Narcissists are often envious of others' successes or accomplishments and may try to undermine them. They may also believe that others are envious of them, even when there's no evidence to support this.
- They often minimize the achievements of others, making it clear that they see themselves as superior.

Examples:

- Dismissing someone's promotion or accomplishment as unimportant or undeserved.
- Speaking negatively about others behind their backs to diminish their success.

7. Inflated Ego Coupled with Fragile Self-Esteem

- While narcissists project confidence and superiority, their self-esteem is often fragile. They are highly sensitive to criticism and may react with defensiveness, anger, or even rage when their self-image is threatened.
- They may lash out at anyone who they perceive as undermining them, even if the feedback is constructive or minor.

Examples:

- Becoming angry or defensive when given even mild criticism.
- Responding to perceived slights with extreme anger or by cutting someone out of their life.

8. Idealization and Devaluation in Relationships

- In the early stages of a relationship, narcissists often idealize their partners, showering them with affection and attention. However, this is usually short-lived, and they soon begin to devalue the person, finding faults or withdrawing affection.
- This cycle of idealization and devaluation can be emotionally confusing and damaging to those involved.

Examples:

- Showering someone with attention early on, only to become critical or distant once the person is committed to the relationship.
- Elevating someone as "perfect" one day and tearing them down the next.

9. Manipulation and Control

- Narcissists often use manipulation to maintain control over others. This can take the form of emotional manipulation, guilt-tripping, gaslighting, or making others feel responsible for the narcissist's feelings.
- They may also use charm or flattery to get what they want, only to discard or devalue the person once they've served their purpose.

Examples:

- Gaslighting: making someone doubt their perception of reality by denying things that happened or manipulating facts.
- Guilt-tripping: making someone feel guilty for not meeting their demands or expectations.

10. Superficial Charm

- Many narcissists can be very charming and charismatic, especially at first. They know how to win people over with their confidence, humor, and social skills.
- However, this charm is often superficial, and over time, the narcissist's self-centeredness and lack of genuine care for others become apparent.

Examples:

- Being the life of the party or effortlessly winning people over, only to show little true interest or care in maintaining deep connections.
- Using charm to manipulate people into liking or trusting them before taking advantage of them.

11. Blaming Others

- Narcissists rarely take responsibility for their actions, especially when things go wrong. They tend to shift blame onto others, avoiding accountability and painting themselves as the victim.
- When confronted about their behavior, they may react with anger or defensiveness, often accusing others of being too sensitive or unfair.

Examples:

- Blaming others for their failures or shortcomings.
- Refusing to apologize or take accountability when they hurt someone.

12. Difficulty Handling Criticism or Failure

- Narcissists often react disproportionately to criticism or failure. They may respond with anger, aggression, or extreme defensiveness.
- Even minor setbacks can cause them significant distress because they threaten their inflated sense of self-worth.

Examples:

- Overreacting to constructive criticism by attacking the person offering it.
- Denying responsibility when they make mistakes or reframing the situation to make it seem like someone else's fault.

Conclusion

Identifying narcissistic behavior requires paying attention to consistent patterns of manipulation, entitlement, and lack of empathy. Narcissists can often mask their more harmful traits with charm and confidence, especially early in relationships, but over time, their behavior reveals their true motivations. Recognizing these traits can help individuals protect themselves from emotional abuse and manipulation by setting boundaries or seeking support when needed.

How to Safely Escape an Abusive Relationship: A Step-by-Step Guide

This guide outlines practical steps to help you leave safely and start the process of rebuilding your life.

Escaping an abusive relationship requires careful planning, support, and strategic action, especially when there's a risk of physical harm.

Escaping an abusive relationship is a courageous step, and it can feel overwhelming, but you don't have to do it alone. Building a support network, planning carefully, and taking the necessary precautions can help ensure your safety and well-being as you move forward into a healthier and more secure future. Remember: you deserve a life free from abuse, and help is available.

Step 1: Acknowledge the Abuse

Before anything else, you must acknowledge that you are in an abusive relationship. Abuse can take many forms—physical, emotional, psychological, financial, or sexual. Accepting that the behavior is harmful is the first step toward freeing yourself.

- Common signs of abuse: controlling behavior, isolation, threats, humiliation, physical harm, and gaslighting.
- Important: Abuse is never your fault, and you deserve to be safe and respected.

Step 2: Build a Support System

It's essential to reach out to trusted people who can offer emotional and practical support. Isolation is a common tactic abusers use to maintain control, so reconnecting with others is vital.

- Tell someone you trust: Reach out to a friend, family member, or coworker and explain your situation.
- Seek professional support: Contact domestic violence hotlines or shelters. They can provide counseling, legal assistance, and temporary housing if needed.
  - U.S. Domestic Violence Hotline: 1-800-799-SAFE (7233)
  - International Resources: Look for local hotlines or support organizations specific to your country or region.
- Join a support group: Hearing from others who've experienced similar situations can be empowering.

Step 3: Prepare a Safety Plan

If you're in immediate danger or believe the situation could escalate, it's critical to have a safety plan in place. This plan will ensure you can leave quickly and safely when the time is right.

- Pack an emergency bag: Include essential items such as:
    - Identification (ID, driver's license, passport)
    - Birth certificates (yours and your children's)
    - Important documents (medical records, financial documents, legal paperwork)
    - Spare cash, debit/credit cards
    - A few days worth of clothes and medications
    - A phone charger
    - Keep this bag hidden but easily accessible.
- Identify a safe place to go: Whether it's a friend's home, family member's house, or a domestic violence shelter, know where you will go once you leave.
- Have an escape route: Know the safest way out of your home, and practice leaving without drawing attention.
- Create a code word: Establish a code word with a trusted friend or family member that signals when you are in danger and need help immediately.

Step 4: Gather Financial Resources

If the abuser controls the finances, you'll need to take steps toward financial independence. Start slowly and discreetly.

- Open a separate bank account: If possible, open a new bank account in your name and ensure your partner cannot access it. Use this account to save money if you can.
- Save money secretly: Try to save cash, even in small amounts, and keep it hidden or stored with someone you trust.
- Explore financial aid options: Many domestic violence shelters offer temporary financial assistance. Additionally, some nonprofits or local organizations can help with housing, legal fees, or other expenses.

Step 5: Plan Your Exit

Planning your exit carefully is crucial, as leaving an abusive partner can be dangerous. The moment you leave is often the most risky because the abuser may escalate their behavior to regain control.

- Pick the right time: Leave when your partner is away or distracted. Avoid confrontations if possible.

- Inform your support network: Let friends, family, or a domestic violence counselor know when and how you plan to leave. They can provide backup and ensure someone is ready to help.
- Avoid leaving clues: Be mindful of your search history, text messages, or any changes in routine that could raise suspicion.
    - Important: If you believe your partner is monitoring your devices, use a trusted friend's phone or computer to plan your escape.

Step 6: Take Legal Precautions

Once you have left, it may be necessary to take legal steps to protect yourself and your children if applicable.

- Obtain a restraining order: Depending on the laws in your area, a restraining or protective order can help prevent the abuser from contacting you or coming near your home or workplace.
- Consult with a lawyer: If you need help with divorce proceedings, child custody, or dividing assets, a lawyer can advise you on your legal rights and options.
- Inform law enforcement: If you fear immediate danger, contact the police for assistance and document any threats or instances of abuse.

Step 7: Secure Your New Life

After leaving, focus on securing your safety and rebuilding your life. Here are some important steps to consider:

- Cut contact with the abuser: Block their phone number, social media accounts, and email. If you must communicate due to shared children or legal matters, do so through a lawyer or third-party intermediary.
- Change passwords: Update all your online passwords, including email, social media, and financial accounts.
- Alert your workplace: If necessary, inform your employer about the situation. They can help ensure your safety at work, such as screening visitors or changing your schedule.
- Consider relocating: In some cases, moving to a new city or state may be the best option for long-term safety.

Resources and Hotlines

- National Domestic Violence Hotline (U.S.): 1-800-799-7233
- National Coalition Against Domestic Violence: www.ncadv.org
- International Domestic Violence Resources: Look for local shelters, helplines, and support networks in your country.
- The Healing Circle www.thehealingcircleorg.com

To all the incredible women who shared their stories with such openness and transparency, I am deeply grateful. Your courage to speak your truth and your willingness to let others into your journey have been both inspiring and empowering. Your voices remind us of the strength in vulnerability, the power of community, and the importance of supporting one another.

Thank you for your honesty, your bravery, and your trust. You have made a lasting impact, and i honor each of you for the strength and resilience you've shown.
With sincere appreciation,

Felicia Carr

Made in the USA
Columbia, SC
07 November 2024

45345635R00046